South Devon

An area of rolling hillsides, granite moorland, thatched cottages and _____ Devon is a popular holiday destination. Inland, lies wild and remote _____ and sparkling streams spanned by ancient bridges are scattered across the rugged and forbidding moorland scenery and sturdy ponies roam free in all weathers. On the mild south coast where sub-tropical plants grow, the resorts which line Tor Bay have justly earned the title of "Devon Riviera". The South Hams district encompasses some of the most diverse and enchanting scenery in the county. Panoramic coastal views embrace sheltered estuaries beloved by yachtsmen, picturesque coves, quiet fishing villages and bustling ports. With their long maritime tradition, the proud history of South Devon's seaports such as Dartmouth and Plymouth is also the history of England.

Around Plymouth

Superbly situated on a broad estuary, **Plymouth** is a fascinating city with a maritime tradition that goes back 700 years. The oldest part of the city is the area around Sutton Harbour *(below left)* with its cobbled alleyways and ancient quays. It was from here that the voyages of Drake, Raleigh and many other Elizabethan seafarers began. Although plans for a bridge across the River Tamar were discussed in the 1820s, it was not until 1961 that the Tamar Road Bridge was finally opened to traffic. Beside it, carrying the railway from Devon into Cornwall, stands the Royal Albert Bridge, which was designed by Isambard Kingdom Brunel and opened by the Prince Consort in 1859.

The Hoe, where Drake played his famous game of bowls before putting to sea against the Armada, commands panoramic views of Plymouth Sound. It is dominated by Smeaton's Tower *(below)* which served as part of the Eddystone Lighthouse from 1759 to 1882. When its foundations began to crumble it was dismantled and brought ashore to be re-erected on the Hoe slopes .

To the north of Plymouth is the busy market town of **Tavistock**, western gateway to Dartmoor. In the Middle Ages it was an important wool town, and the local tin and copper mining industries added to its prosperity over the years. The town stands on the River Tavy which is spanned by the fine old Abbey Bridge *(above)*. Standing in a landscaped park overlooking Plymouth Sound, **Saltram House** *(right)* contains some notable furniture, china and pictures. It dates originally from the Tudor period but it was extended and redesigned in Georgian times.

Buckland Abbey *(left)* was originally founded by the Cistercian order in 1278, and was one of the religious houses which was transformed for domestic use after the Dissolution of the Monasteries by Henry VIII. First owned by the Grenvilles, it was bought in 1581 by Sir Francis Drake. Now preserved by The National Trust, the house contains relics and exhibitions about the exploits and achievements of both great seamen.

The South Hams

The South Hams district stretches from the River Dart to the Cornish border, and from Dartmoor in the north to Prawle Point, the southernmost point on the Devon coast. It encompasses some of the most diverse and enchanting scenery in the county. South-east of Plymouth the pretty River Yealm makes its way between wooded slopes to the sea where it flows into **Wembury Bay** *(right)*. The Great Mew Stone is a prominent landmark in the bay. The waterside village of **Noss Mayo** *(below)* is delightfully situated on an arm of the River Yealm. On the other side of the richly wooded creek, sharing the harbour, is its sister village of **Newton Ferrers**.

Ivybridge *(left)* takes its name from the picturesque 13th century humpbacked bridge which spans the River Erme. This attractive little town gives access to the western part of Dartmoor and is also a good centre for some delightful walks following the twists and turns of the river through the beautiful scenery of the South Hams.

Nearby **Modbury** *(right)* is a delightful small town reached along the narrow lanes, flanked by high hedges and banks of wild flowers, which are typical of the South Hams scenery. It boasts a number of interesting old buildings, many of them slate-hung, a characteristic feature of the area. The church was rebuilt in the 17th century but, unusually in Devon, it has a medieval spire.

The undulating hills of the South Hams provide superb walking country. Around **Erme Mouth** *(left)* they slope down to meet some fine sandy beaches. The estuary is noted for its birdlife. Redshank, dunlin, oystercatchers, curlew and turnstones can be seen on the sandflats, whilst stonechats, whitethroats and linnets frequent the cliffs.

There are many small resorts and quaint villages in the delightful South Hams district. **Bigbury-on-Sea** *(above)* is a lively holiday hamlet with a sandy beach which sweeps round towards the mouth of the River Avon. Offshore lies tiny Burgh Island which can be reached on foot at low tide or by means of an unusual sea tractor at high water. Here the Pilchard Inn *(right)* dates from the 14th century when a monastic community lived on the island. Pilchard fishing was a major industry here at one time and near the inn stands a ruined hut from where look-outs used to scan Bigbury Bay, watching for the shoals of pilchards to arrive. It is said that the inn was once a base for smugglers who brought their contraband ashore along this coast. Nearby **Bantham** *(right)*, a tiny port on the banks of the River Avon, was once busy with coasters unloading their cargoes to be transported up the River Avon.

The village of **Thurlestone**, with its magnificent sandy beaches *(above)*, faces west across the Bigbury Bay and at low tide it is possible to walk out to the Thurlestone Rock *(below)*, an isolated natural arch of rock worn away by the action of the sea. Nearby, the attractive village of **Ringmore** *(left)*, with its its fine thatched cottages, is typical of many that give the area its distinctive Old-world charm.

Picturesque **Hope Cove** *(left)* is a small bay of sand and rock nestling under the cliffs of Bolt Tail which offers shelter for a little harbour. Here, at the end of the day, boats are drawn up onto the beach. The village *(below)* also boasts a number of the quaint cob-walled and thatched cottages which are characteristic of traditional West Country building styles. The walls, which consist of layers of earth, straw and cow hair, are often two or three feet thick.

The principal town in the South Hams is the ancient market town of **Kingsbridge** *(left)*. Fore Street rises steeply up from the quayside, lined with fascinating old shops including the 16th century Shambles. At the top stands the splendid 15th century church. Here the sheltered waters are ideal for small boats, and in summer the estuary is crowded with pleasure craft of all kinds.

With one of the finest natural harbours in the West Country, **Salcombe** is the gateway to a vast network of tidal creeks and inlets. Small boats are able to explore the river as far inland as Kingsbridge and a regatta has been held here ever since the 1850s. As well as being a popular haven for yachtsmen, holiday-makers are attracted to Salcombe by its mild climate, splendid cliff scenery and sandy beaches.

Start Bay sweeps southward from the pretty little wooded cove of **Blackpool Sands** *(above)* for some eight miles. In the centre of this panoramic sweep is **Slapton Sands** *(facing)*, with the small seaside village of **Torcross** at its southern end. This popular sand and shingle beach was used as a practice area for the Normandy invasion in 1944. Separated from the sea by a long bank of shingle is **Slapton Ley** *(below)*, a freshwater lake about two miles in length which is designated a site of special scientific interest due to its abundant wildlife. **Start Point** *(right)* is one of the most exposed peninsulas on the English coast, extending for almost a mile into the sea on the south side of the bay. For 170 years the lighthouse has stood at the end of the bracken-covered headland, warning shipping away from dangerous rocks and shingle banks.

Dartmouth and the River Dart

Rising in the heart of Dartmoor, the River Dart is one of Devon's principal rivers. It flows through rolling, wooded countryside until it reaches the sea between Dartmouth and Kingswear, two places linked by a ferry since 1365. **Dartmouth,** a town whose seafaring traditions go back to the 12th century when crusaders set sail from here, is situated on the western side of the estuary. With its cobbled quay and Tudor fort, Bayard's Cove *(below left)* is probably the oldest part of this ancient port. From here in 1620 the *Mayflower* and the *Speedwell* set sail carrying the Pilgrim Fathers to the New World. A plaque at the entrance to Bayard's Cove commemorates their departure. Offering superb views at the mouth of the river, Dartmouth Castle *(below right)* was built in 1481 to defend the town against raids from the sea. It was positioned opposite Kingswear Castle so that in times of war a chain could be stretched between the two forts preventing boats from sailing up the estuary.

Situated in a beautiful valley on the coast near Kingswear is **Coleton Fishacre** *(left)*. The sheltered garden has streams, ponds, a gazebo and a fine collection of rare and exotic plants, including some superb bamboos and mimosas.

The pretty village of **Dittisham** *(right)*, where Sir Walter Raleigh used to spend boyhood holidays, is surrounded by attractive wooded scenery beside a bend in the River Dart. Here neat cottages cluster above the quay from where a passenger ferry crosses the river. A little further inland is the unspoilt village of **Stoke Gabriel** *(bottom)*, with its ancient inns and cottages. Nestling on a creek of the River Dart, it is a popular spot for fishing and also a good centre for walks.

Following the line of the old Great Western Railway from Totnes to Buckfastleigh, the **South Devon Railway** *(right)* meanders through the pastoral undulating, wooded landscape of the lovely Dart Valley for some seven miles.

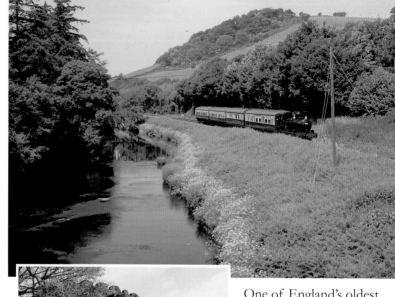

One of England's oldest boroughs and an important settlement in Saxon times, **Totnes** has many fine buildings, and a castle *(left)* built by the Normans to guard the river crossing. The restored 15th century East Gate *(far left)* in Fore Street is one of two gateways which remain from medieval times when Totnes was a walled town. The fine church *(below)* with its impressive tower is Norman in origin. Beside it stands the Guildhall, a wonderfully preserved 16th century building which houses the old jail and a table where Oliver Cromwell sat in 1646.

A 14th century tilt-yard and its terraces are at the heart of the magnificent restored gardens at **Dartington Hall** *(above)*. Walkways through bay, yew and holly plantings provide a contrasting background for flowering trees and shrubs such as camellias, magnolias and rhododendrons. Standing on a wooded cliff near Totnes, the great three-storeyed Norman gatehouse with its imposing hexagonal towers is all that remains of **Berry Pomeroy Castle** *(right)*.

Buckfast Abbey *(left)* lies in a fertile valley beside the River Dart on the south-eastern edge of Dartmoor. It was a very early foundation which was well established by the reign of King Canute. In common with many other religious houses, it fell into ruin after the Dissolution of the Monasteries, but in the 1880s the present magnificent structure was built on the original foundations.

The English Riviera

With its magnificent resorts surrounding Tor Bay and its mild climate, that part of the Devon coast which lies between the Rivers Exe and Dart has come to be known as the English Riviera. The popular holiday resort of **Brixham** has been a major fishing port for 300 years and its safe, accessible harbour is still busy with yachts and small craft of all kinds. A full-size replica of the *Golden Hind*, in which Sir Francis Drake sailed round the world, is moored there and a statue on the quay commemorates the landing in 1688 of Prince William of Orange, the future William III.

Lying in the centre of the magnificent sweep of Tor Bay, **Paignton** *(above)* is one of the premier resorts in this area. It has a fine, mile-long stretch of sand and a small but busy harbour. The **Paignton and Dartmouth Steam Railway** *(left)* runs for seven miles through superb scenery along the spectacular Torbay coast between Paignton and Kingswear, stopping at **Churston** *(left)* and **Goodrington**. For the more energetic, it is also possible to walk this stretch of coast on the South West Coast Path which leads from Paignton through Goodrington Sands to the pretty little beach at **Elberry Cove** *(bottom)*.

Described by Alfred Lord Tennyson as "the loveliest sea village in England", **Torquay** is built on the hillside overlooking beautiful Tor Bay. Visitors have flocked to the area since the late 18th century and Torquay, aptly known as the "Queen of the English Riviera", has a delightful Mediterranean atmosphere with its profusion of subtropical plants and its busy harbour full of small boats. Dame Agatha Christie, one of the most famous mystery and crime writers of all time, was born in Torquay in 1890. She later returned to spend her honeymoon at the Grand Hotel in the town.

Jutting out into the huge, sand-rimmed bay is a line of three rocky islets, the largest of which is known as the Thatcher Rock *(above)* because of its distinctive green "thatch". Nearby bustling Torquay, the quaint hamlet of **Cockington** *(left)* is the epitome of the peaceful rural charm of Old England. The ancient thatched forge and cob-walled cottages attract many visitors including artists and photographers. Cockington Court *(below)*, which now houses a craft centre, was rebuilt in 1679 and it was at this time that the extensive gardens were created. This beautiful, walled rose garden provides a sheltered, sunny spot in which to enjoy a few moments of tranquillity.

Babbacombe, once a more bustling and popular resort than nearby Torquay, is set on a gentle curving bay. A steep hill descends from Babbacombe Downs to the crescent-shaped, sandy beach, which is protected by a little stone quay. Neighbouring Oddicombe Beach *(above)* is sheltered by high cliffs comprising of an attractive mixture of red sandstone and pale limestone. The sands can be reached by means of a cliff railway. There are pleasant walks along the cliff-top from where it is possible to see Portland Bill, forty miles away.

Standing on the wide River Teign estuary, **Teignmouth** *(above and below)* is one of the Devon Riviera resorts known for its mild climate and superb situation. With its handsome esplanade, beautifully kept gardens and a colourful riverside harbour from which Dartmoor granite was once shipped, Teignmouth has long been popular with visitors. Separated from Teignmouth by the estuary of the River Teign, the sheltered resort of **Shaldon** *(right)* stands beneath a wooded headland known as The Ness. Popular as a yachting centre, Shaldon also offers fishing and beaches of sand and shingle.

Lying between the Rivers Exe and Teign is the charming seaside town of **Dawlish** where novelist Charles Dickens set part of *Nicholas Nickleby*. On its way to the sea, attractive Dawlish Water, known locally as The Stream *(inset, bottom)*, flows over a series of small weirs through The Lawn, a delightful little park inhabited by black swans and some rare species of ducks and geese. Dawlish has a long beach of sand and fine shingle. At one end of the beach high cliffs shelter a little cove where small boats are often pulled ashore. A coastal path links Dawlish and neighbouring **Dawlish Warren** *(inset, below)* where a nature reserve protects many plant species as well as resident wading birds and winter migrants.

Built over 600 years ago, **Powderham Castle** *(right)* is the historic home of the Earls of Devon. Set in an ancient deer park alongside the River Exe, the castle reflects the many changes which have taken place since medieval times including the destruction and rebuilding occasioned by the Civil War, and the elegant additions made in the 17th and 18th centuries.

Situated on the main road between Dartmouth and Exeter, **Newton Abbot** *(left)* has been a busy market town since medieval times. The sturdy tower is all that now remains of St. Leonard's Church, built in 1350. The town expanded rapidly when the railway arrived in the 1840s, becoming a centre for the Great Western Railway.

Shortly before it joins the Teign, the River Bovey flows through **Bovey Tracey** *(right)*, eastern gateway to Dartmoor and also within easy reach of the Devon Riviera resorts. This attractive small town is noted for its fine church which is believed to have been built in honour of Thomas à Becket by the de Tracey family who gave their name to the town and whose ancestors were implicated in the murder of the saint.

Historic Exeter

Founded by the Romans, **Exeter** is a fascinating city with many beautiful old buildings which testify to its long and important history. One of the most intriguing structures in the city is the "House that Moved" *(top)*. It is thought to be one of the oldest timber-framed houses in Europe. This 15th century merchant's house was moved intact in 1961 from its original site to its present position near the River Exe opposite the Church of St. Mary Steps. At one time much of Exeter's prosperity came from the wool trade and the quays and warehouses on the banks of the river testify to the town's importance as a port. The Custom House *(middle)* was built in 1681 and was one of the first buildings in Exeter to be constructed in brick. Mol's Coffee House *(bottom)* stands under the shadow of the cathedral. This fine 16th century building was a popular meeting place for many famous Elizabethan sea captains. Among the other outstanding buildings in the city is the Guildhall which dates from at least 1160 and is claimed to be the oldest municipal building in the country.

Still used by pleasure boats, the Exeter Ship Canal is one of the oldest waterways in the country. It was built in 1566 to provide a navigable route into Exeter when the River Exe was closed by a weir. At Turf Locks *(right)*, the canal rejoins the river where it widens into a large estuary as it approaches the sea.

Most impressive of Exeter's many beautiful and historic buildings is the magnificent Norman cathedral which was established in 1050, although it was largely rebuilt in 1275. Standing in the tranquil Cathedral Close, the façade of the superb west front *(below)* possesses the largest expanse of 14th century sculpture surviving in England. The nave *(left)* is one of the greatest achievements of English architecture and preserves the world's longest stretch of 14th century Gothic vaulting.

Around Dartmoor

Often described as Southern England's last great wilderness, Dartmoor National Park embraces both rugged moorland with granite outcrops, and soft river valleys. **Widecombe-in-the-Moor** *(right)* is arguably the most famous village on Dartmoor, known for its annual fair which is immortalised in the traditional song *Widecombe Fair*. The massive church is known as the "Cathedral of the Moor" because of its great size. At **Postbridge** *(bottom)* the East Dart River is spanned by one of Dartmoor's ancient clapper bridges, built of enormous granite slabs supported on four piers.

Haytor *(below)*, silhouetted on the crest of the hill 1,490 feet above sea-level, is one of the best known of the rocky outcrops scattered across the moor. It is seen here from the Granite Tramway. In the early 19th century stone was carried in horse-drawn trucks along the tramway from the nearby quarries to a canal in the valley.

A particularly lovely part of
Dartmoor surrounds Dartmeet
where the East and West Dart
Rivers descend from the uplands
and become one river. Here
stands the attractive old fishing
lodge of **Badgers' Holt** *(right)*.
There are some fine walks in the
area through moorland valleys
or along the River Dart which is
a haven for birds such as
dippers, woodpeckers and the
occasional heron.

The high moorland of the Dartmoor National Park is
threaded by numerous pretty little streams and rivers.
The beauty spot of **Becky Falls** *(above)*, where the brook
cascades seventy feet over boulders into a wooded glade,
is particularly impressive after heavy rain when water
pours off the moor down the steep ravine. One of
Dartmoor's best known features, **Bowerman's Nose**
(right) is a distinctive twenty-two feet high pillar of
weathered granite which has been carved into its curious
shape by the wind and rain.

Princetown *(above)*, named after the Prince Regent, is the largest town on the moor and stands 1,400 feet above sea-level. It is best known for its famous prison, but the green provides a pleasant open space in the centre of the town. The small market town of **Chagford** *(right)* was one of the four ancient stannary towns where tin-miners would bring their tin to be weighed, assessed for taxes and sold. It lies amidst some of the most beautiful scenery in the National Park, with open moorland, wooded hills and the lovely Teign Valley all within easy reach.

An excellent centre for exploring the eastern part of Dartmoor, **Moretonhampstead** *(left)* is a small market town with some fine old buildings. Shops and houses are crowded together in the narrow streets and there are some unusual two-storeyed almshouses which were built in 1451 of Dartmoor granite and extended in 1637. The church is a prominent local landmark.